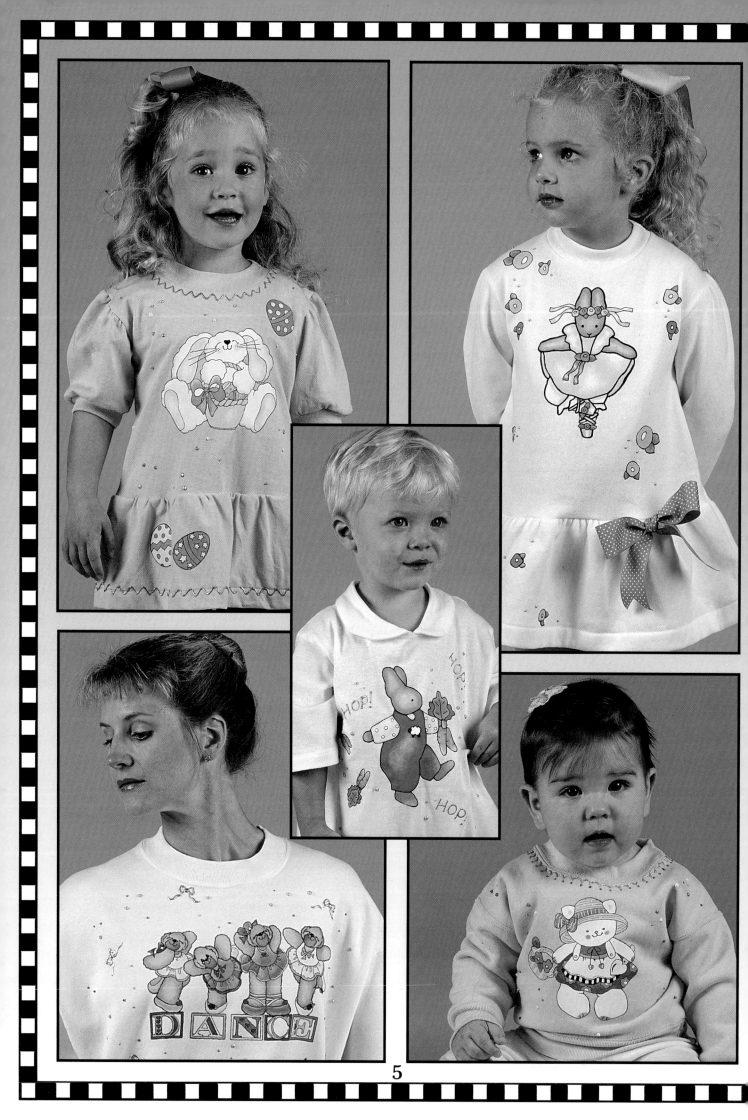

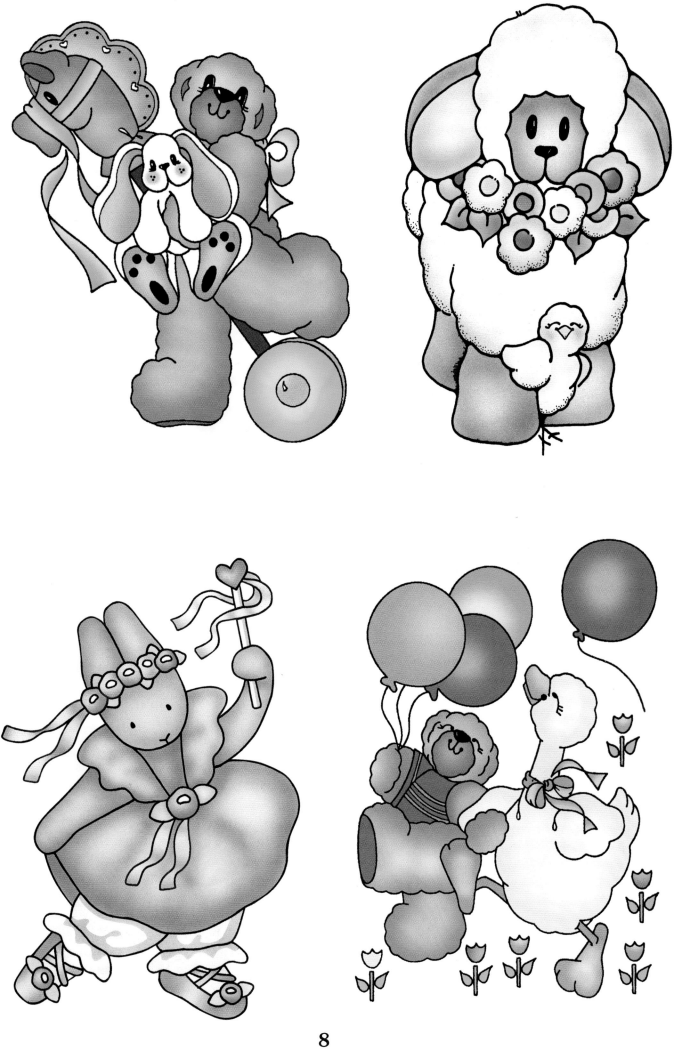

8

10

11

12

16

17

19

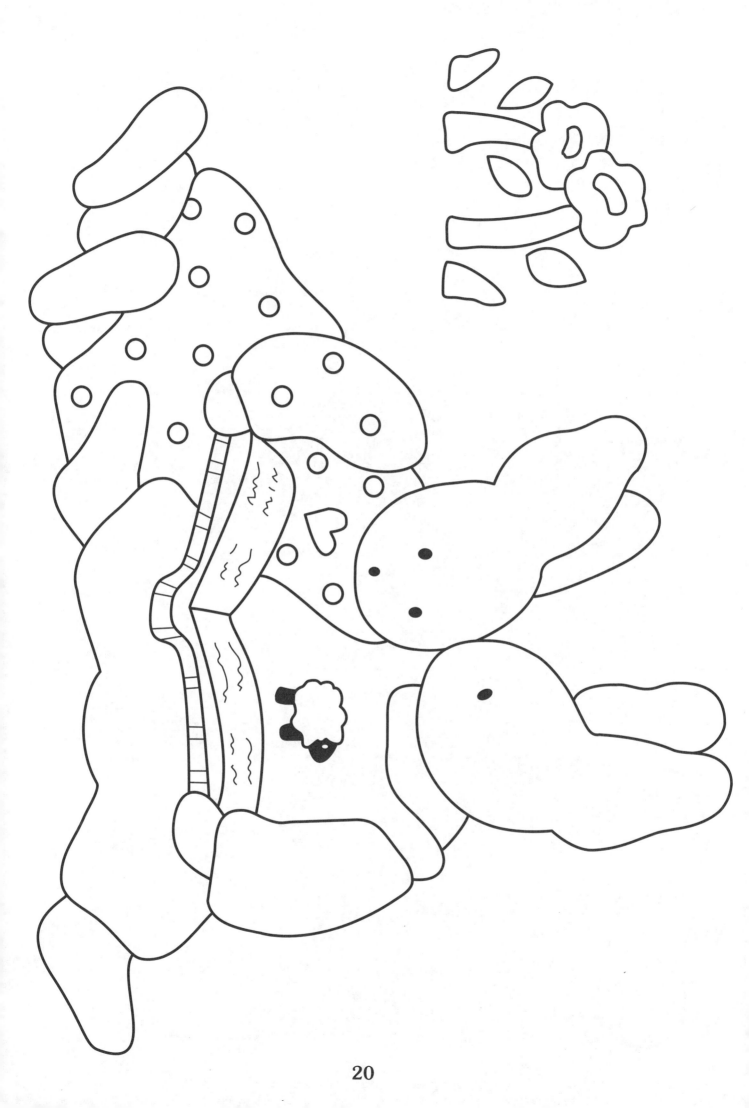

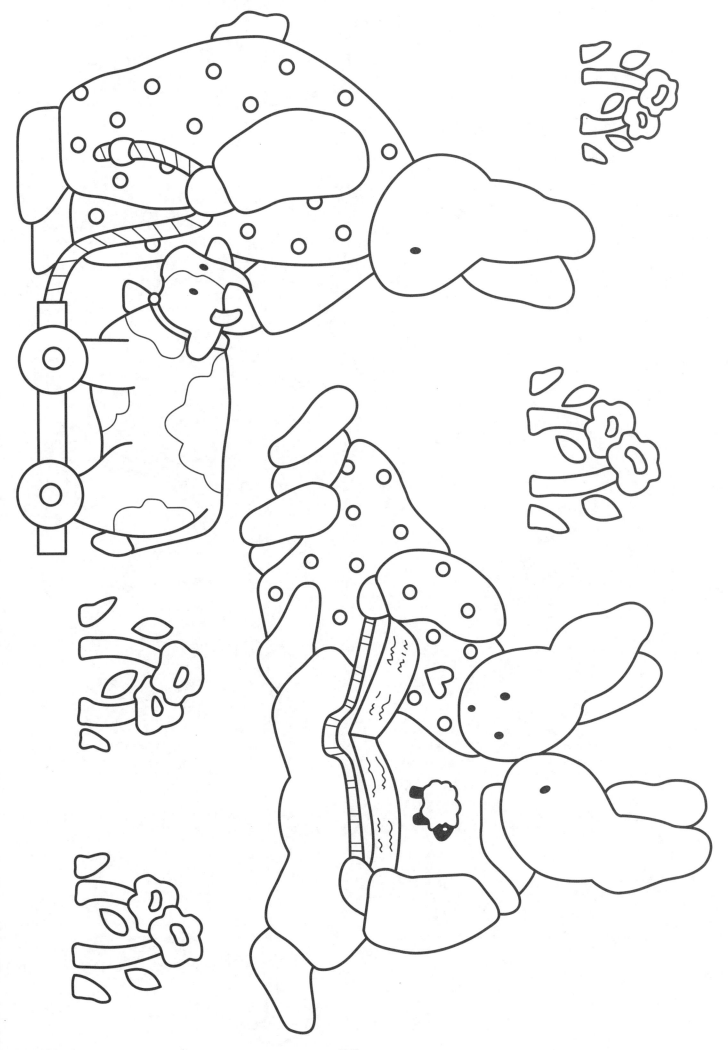

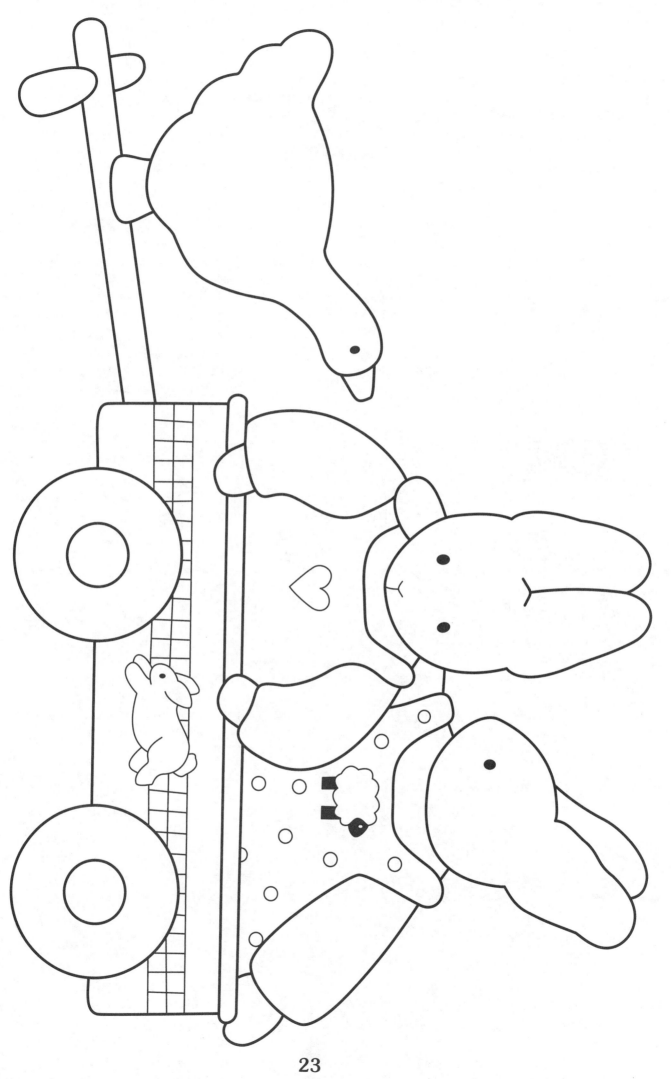

23

24

29

30

34

39

41

44

FRIENDS
ARE FOR
EVER

48

I'm the mama bear
that's why!

51

52

KEEPING HOUSE
IS LIKE THREADING WITH
BEADS ON A STRING WITH
NO KNOT ON THE END...

53

KEEPING HOUSE IS LIKE THREADING BEADS ON A STRING WITH NO KNOT ON THE END.

55

56

59

61

63

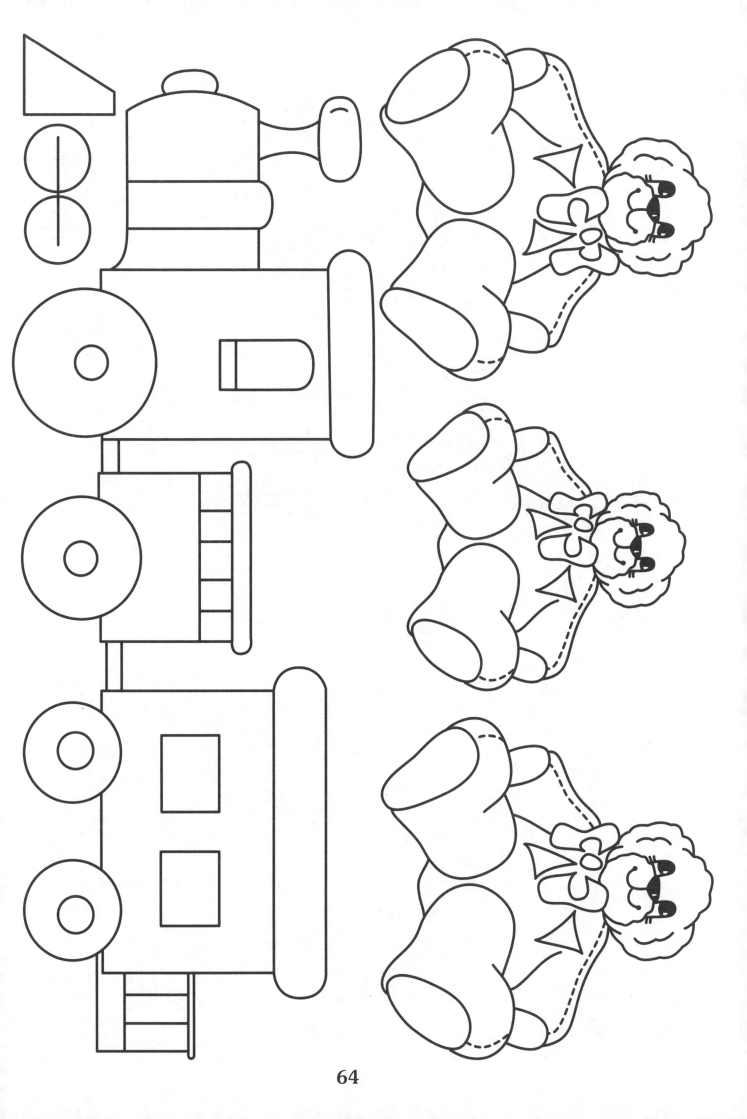

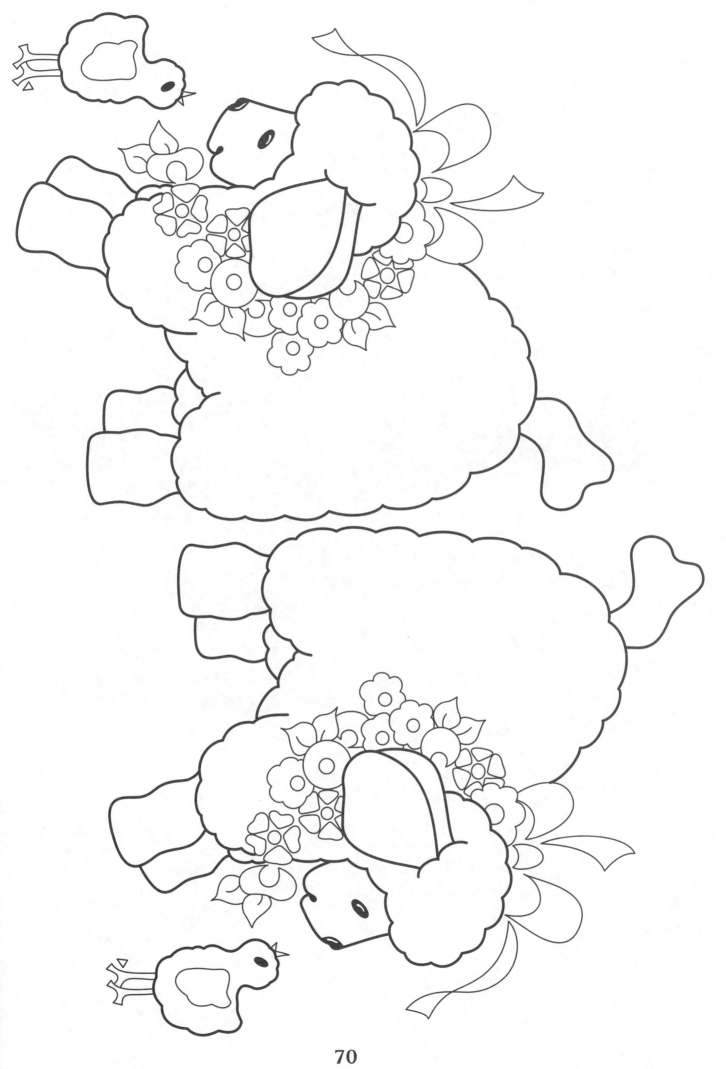

74

EASTER ANGEL

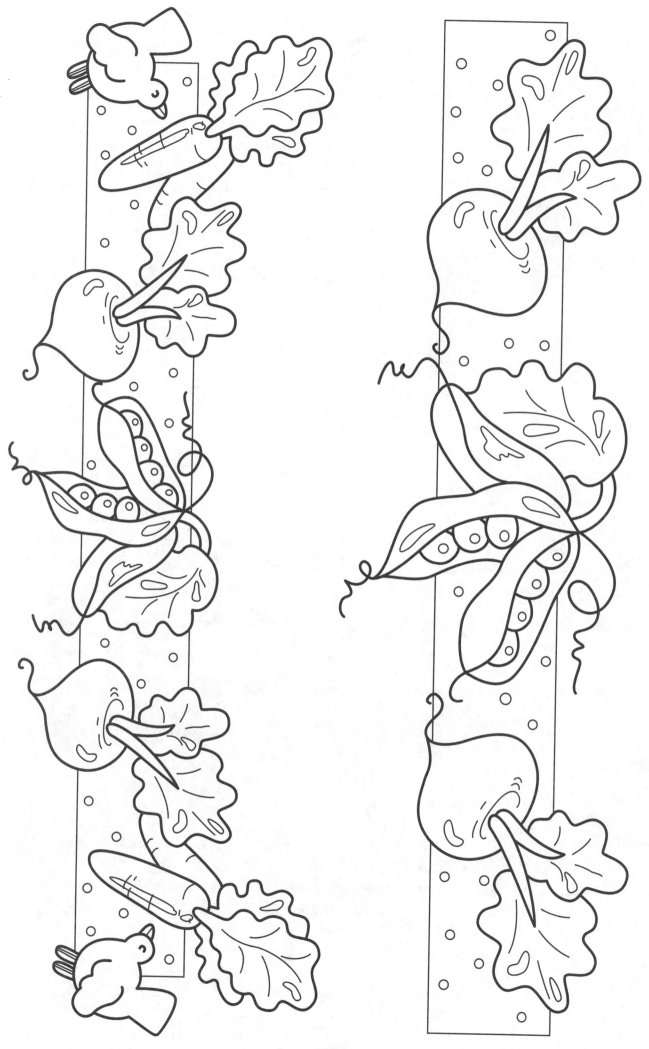

93

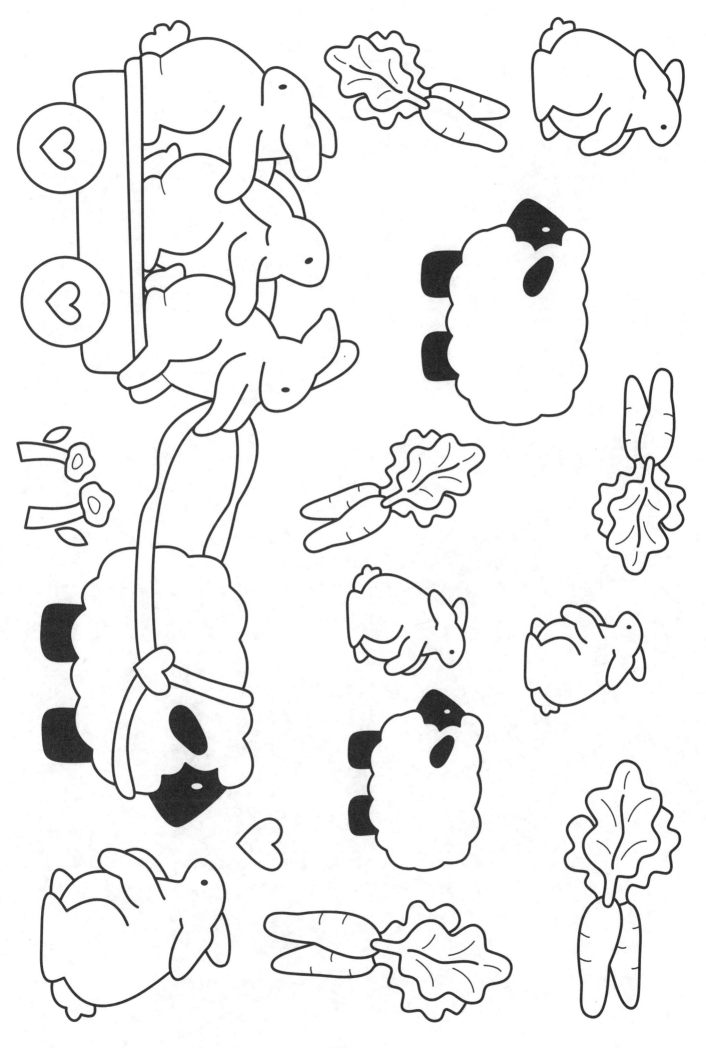

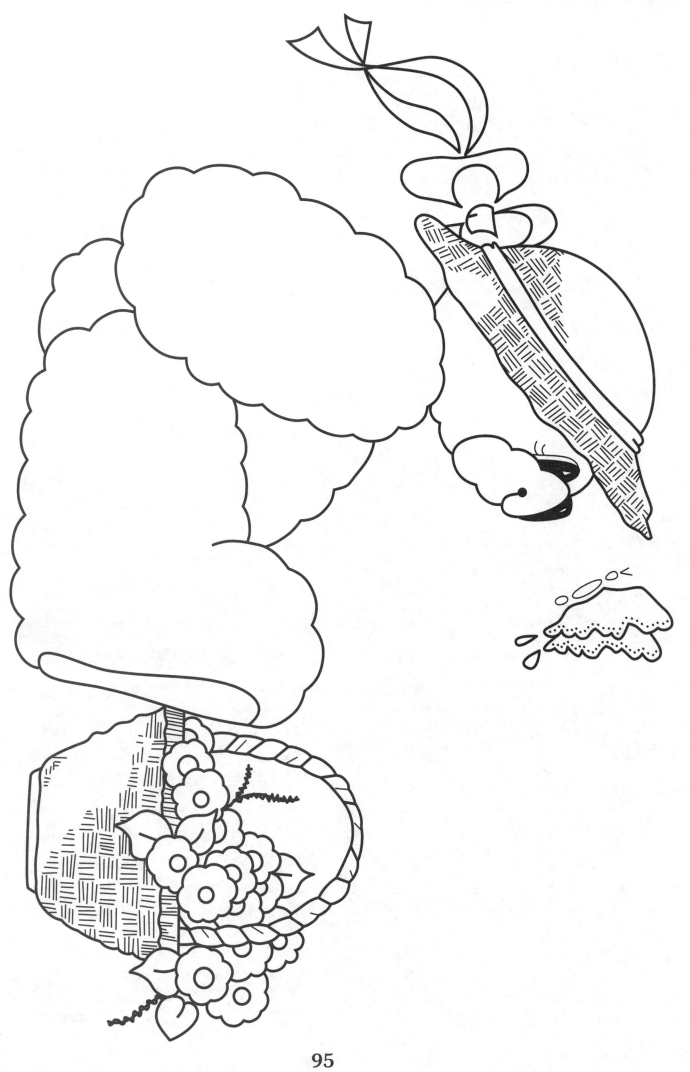

104

105

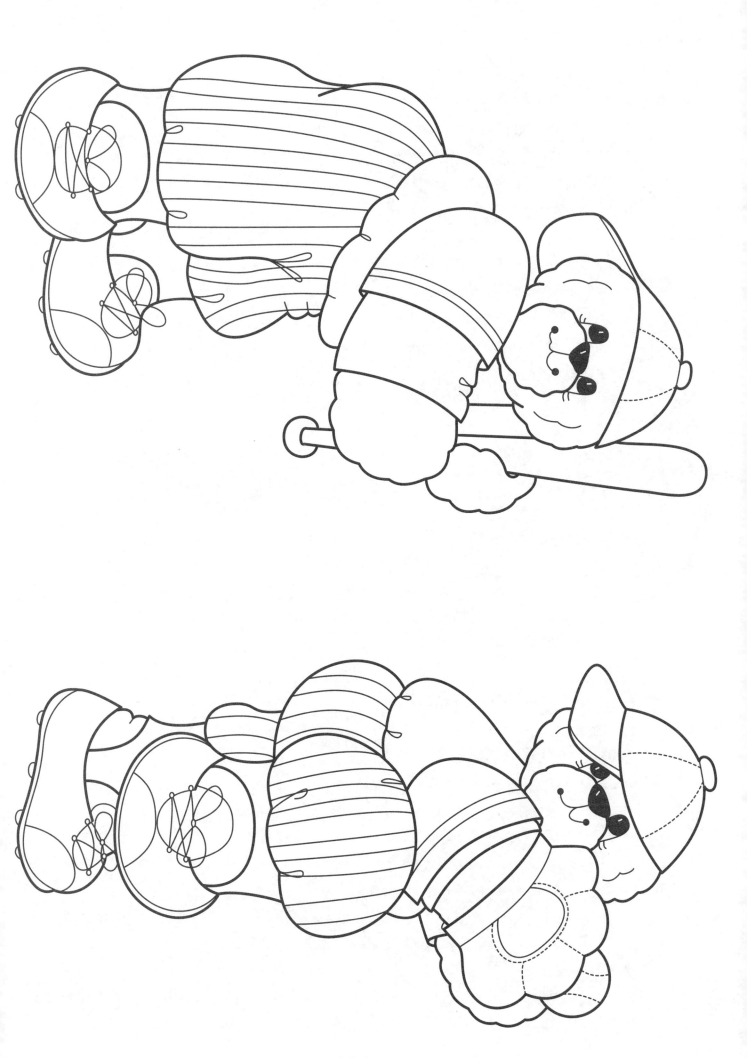

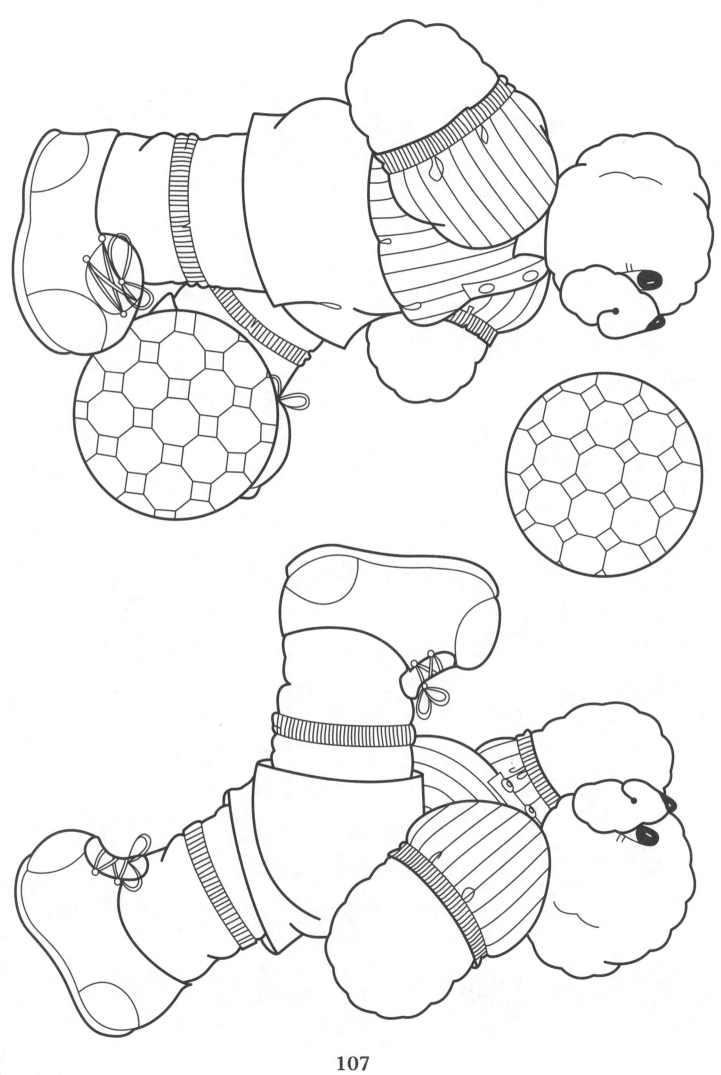

109

CARLETON

Autumn days • Beautiful, golden days • Sweet and smiling you are • HONEY

111

119

121

124

129

130

132

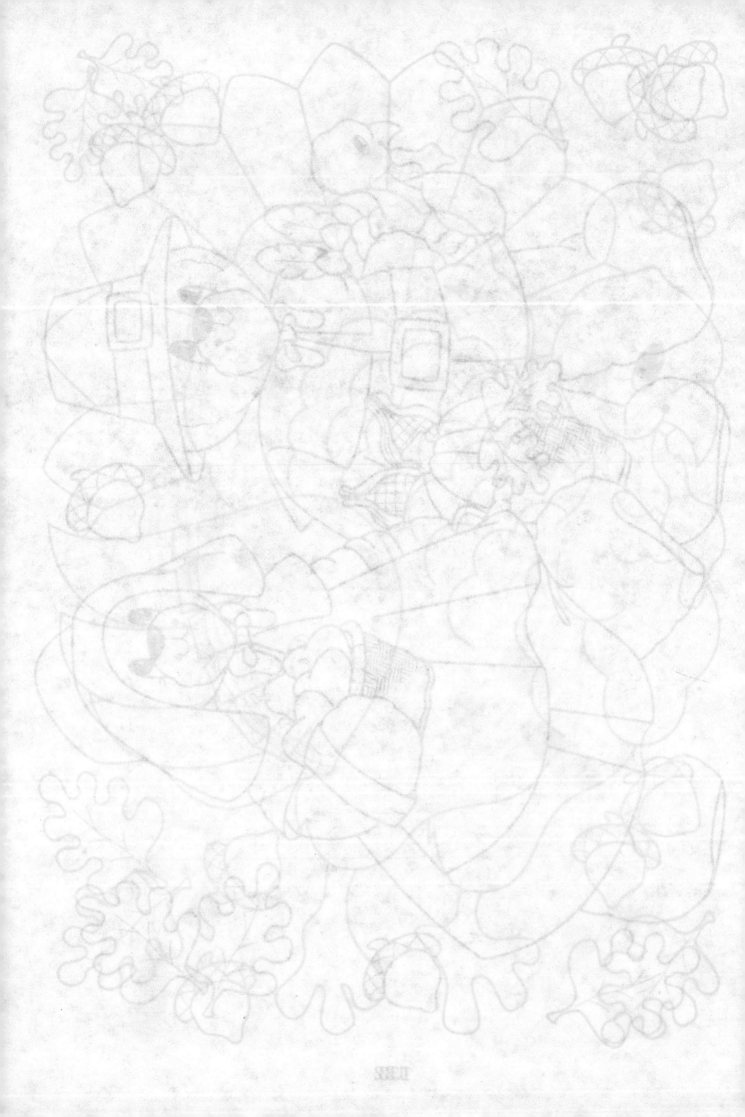

NAUGHTY
SANTA THE TRIP
BE SAVE

137

139

HERE COMES SANTA CLAUS

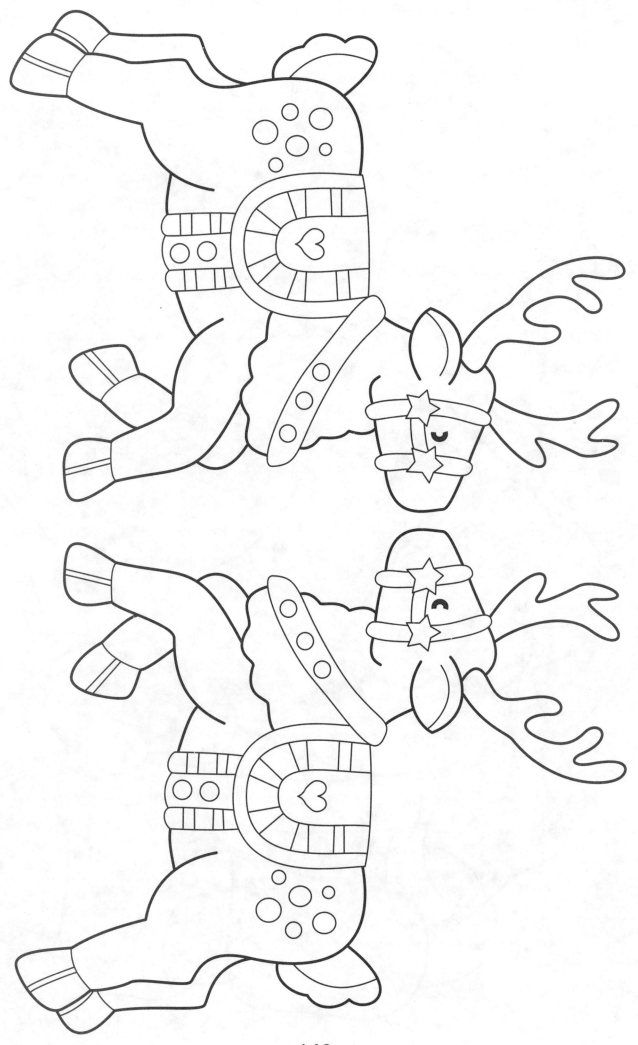

146

148

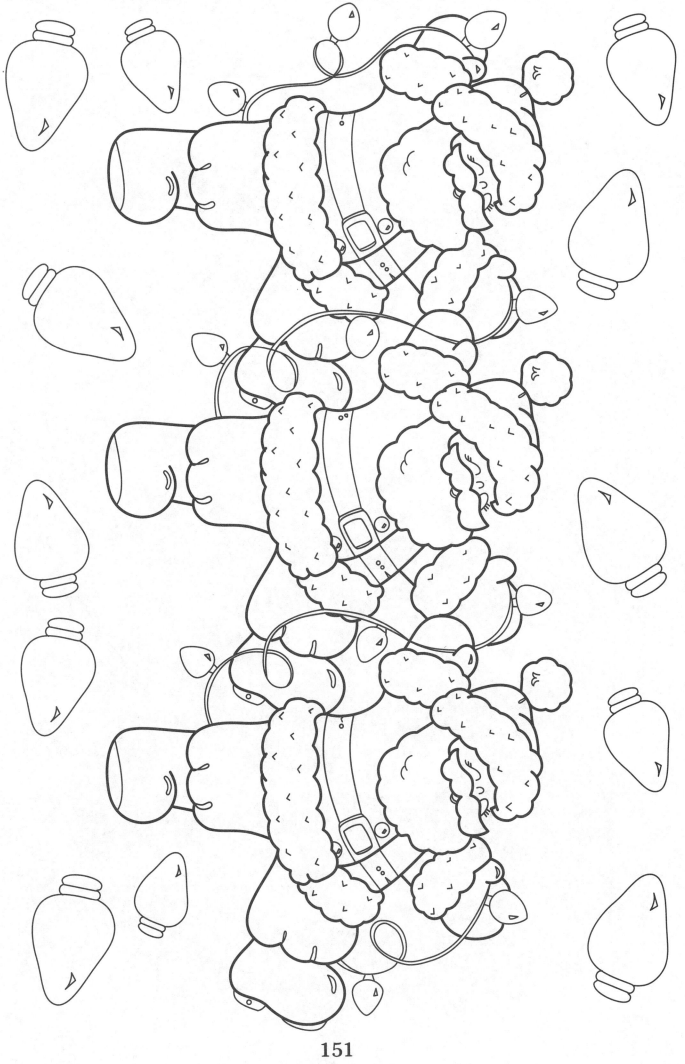

151

153

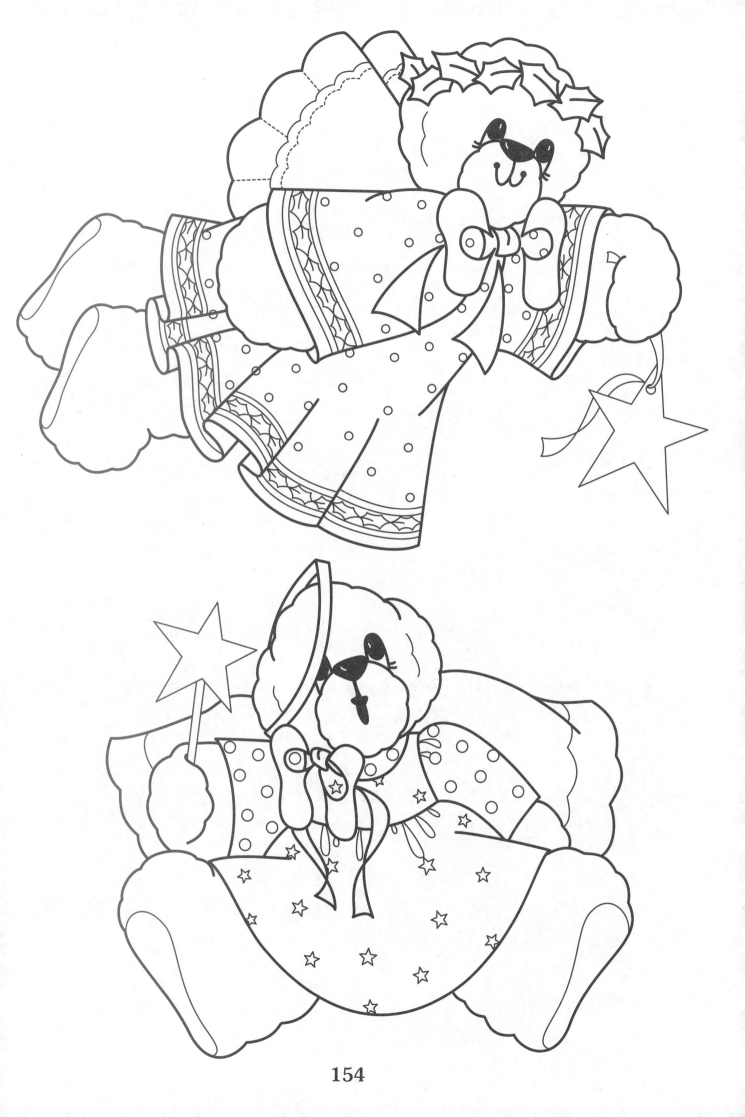

158

160

161

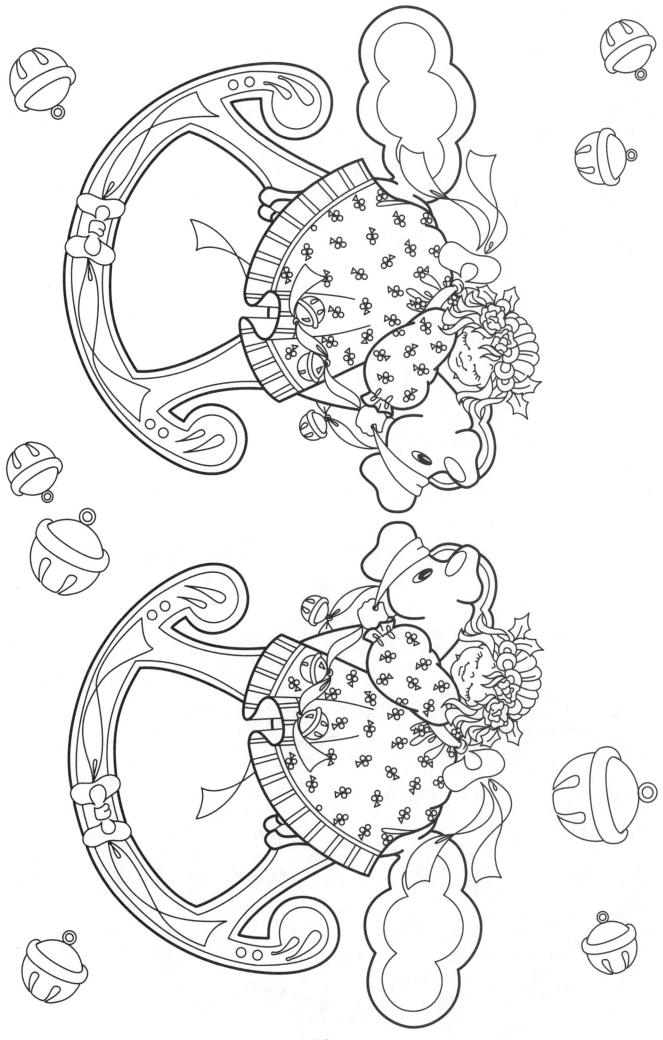

163

169